Our Favorite Pets ❤

Nuestras mascotas favoritas ❤

# Crazy About Puppies

# Locos por los cachorros

Written by / Escrito por: Harold Morris
Translated by / Traducción de: Santiago Ochoa

## TABLE OF CONTENTS



## ÍNDICE



A Crabtree Seedlings Book
Un libro de El Semillero de Crabtree

Crabtree Publishing
crabtreebooks.com

## Puppies

Baby animals are cute!

## Cachorros

¡Los animales bebés son lindos!

Some baby animals, such as baby dogs, make great **pets**.

Algunos animales bebé, como los perros bebé, son excelentes **mascotas**.

Baby dogs are called puppies.

Los perros bebés se llaman cachorros.

puppy (PUHP-ee)
cachorro

litter (LIT-ur)
camada

Some mother dogs may have just one puppy at a time. Others may have many.

Algunas madres pueden tener un solo cachorro a la vez. Otras pueden tener muchos.

**PUPPY FACTS!**

When a mother dog has a group of puppies born at the same time, it is called a **litter** of puppies.

**¡DATOS SOBRE LOS CACHORROS!**

Cuando una madre tiene un grupo de cachorros que nacen al mismo tiempo, se llama una **camada** de cachorros.

A puppy often looks like its mother.

Un cachorro suele parecerse a su madre.

The mother dog takes care of the puppies. She licks them to keep them clean.

La madre cuida a los cachorros. Los lame para mantenerlos limpios.

newborn (NOO-born)
recién nacido

**Newborn** puppies drink milk from their mother. This helps them grow.

Los cachorros **recién nacidos** toman leche de su madre. Esto les ayuda a crecer.

Once puppies grow teeth, they can eat **solid** puppy food.

Cuando a los cachorros les salen los dientes, pueden comer alimentos **sólidos** para cachorros.

Puppies have baby teeth. When their teeth fall out, **adult** teeth grow in their place.

Los cachorros tienen dientes de leche. Cuando se les caen, les crecen dientes de **adulto**.

Dogs and puppies like to chew things.

A los perros y a los cachorros les gusta masticar cosas.

**PUPPY FACTS!**

Chewing dog **treats** helps keep a dog's teeth clean.

**¡DATOS SOBRE LOS CACHORROS!**

Masticar **golosinas** para perros ayuda a mantener limpios sus dientes.

Puppies love to play.
They love to sleep too!

A los cachorros les encanta jugar.
¡También les encanta dormir!

# Glossary / Glosario

**adult** (uh-DUHLT): An adult is a fully grown person or animal.
**adulto:** Un adulto es una persona o un animal completamente desarrollado.

**litter** (LIT-ur): A litter is a group of puppies born to the same mother at the same time.
**camada:** Una camada es un grupo de cachorros nacidos de la misma madre al mismo tiempo.

**newborn** (NOO-born): A newborn is recently born.
**recién nacidos:** Que acaban de nacer.

**pets** (PETS): Pets are animals that people keep and take care of for pleasure.
**mascotas:** Las mascotas son animales que las personas tienen y cuidan por placer.

**solid** (SOL-id): A solid is hard and firm, not runny like a liquid.
**sólidos:** Cosas duras y firmes, que no son fluidas como un líquido.

**treats** (TREETS): Dog treats are made for dogs. Treats are usually given to reward good behavior, or to help clean the dog's teeth.
**golosinas:** Las golosinas para perros están hechas para perros. Las golosinas se suelen dar para premiar el buen comportamiento o para ayudar a limpiar los dientes del perro.

# Index



# Índice analítico

# School-to-Home Support for Caregivers and Teachers

This book helps children grow by letting them practice reading. Here are a few guiding questions to help the reader build his or her comprehension skills. Possible answers appear here in red.

## Before Reading

- **What do I think this book is about?** I think this book is about the funny things that puppies do. I think this book is about how to play with puppies.
- **What do I want to learn about this topic?** I want to learn more about taking care of puppies. I want to learn how old a puppy should be to leave its mother.

## During Reading

- **I wonder why...** I wonder why puppies make great pets. I wonder why some dogs have only one puppy while other dogs have many puppies.
- **What have I learned so far?** I have learned that when a mother dog has a group of puppies born at the same time, we call it a litter of puppies. I have learned that a puppy often looks like its mother.

## After Reading

- **What details did I learn about this topic?** I have learned that the mother dog licks the puppies to keep them clean. I have learned that puppies have baby teeth that fall out and that adult teeth grow in their place.
- **Read the book again and look for the glossary words.** I see the word *litter* on page 9, and the word *treats* on page 20. The other glossary words are found on pages 22 and 23.

# Apoyo escolar para cuidadores y profesores

Este libro ayuda a los niños a crecer permitiéndoles practicar la lectura. A continuación se presentan algunas preguntas orientativas para ayudar al lector a desarrollar su capacidad de comprensión. Las posibles respuestas que aparecen aquí están en color rojo.

## Antes de leer

- **¿De qué creo que trata este libro?** Creo que este libro trata de las cosas divertidas que hacen los cachorros. Creo que este libro trata sobre cómo jugar con los cachorros.
- **¿Qué quiero aprender sobre este tema?** Quiero aprender más sobre el cuidado de los cachorros. Quiero aprender qué edad debe tener un cachorro para dejar a su madre.

## Durante la lectura

- **Me pregunto por qué...** Me pregunto por qué los cachorros son buenas mascotas. Me pregunto por qué algunos perros tienen solo un cachorro mientras que otros tienen muchos.
- **¿Qué he aprendido hasta ahora?** He aprendido que cuando una madre tiene un grupo de cachorros que nacen al mismo tiempo, lo llamamos camada de cachorros. He aprendido que un cachorro suele parecerse a su madre.

## Después de leer

- **¿Qué detalles he aprendido sobre este tema?** He aprendido que la madre lame a los cachorros para mantenerlos limpios. He aprendido que los cachorros tienen dientes de leche que se caen y que en su lugar les crecen dientes adultos.
- **Vuelve a leer el libro y busca las palabras del glosario.** Veo la palabra *camada* en la página 9 y la palabra *golosinas* en la página 20. Las demás palabras del glosario se encuentran en las páginas 22 y 23.

---


**Crabtree Publishing**

crabtreebooks.com 800-387-7650





Hardcover 978-1-0398-6937-0
Paperback 978-1-0398-6916-5
Ebook (pdf) 978-1-0398-6958-5
Epub 978-1-0398-6979-0

**Published in Canada**
**Publicado en Canadá**
**Crabtree Publishing**
616 Welland Avenue
St. Catharines, Ontario
L2M 5V6

**Published in the United States**
**Publicado en los Estados Unidos**
**Crabtree Publishing**
347 Fifth Avenue
Suite 1402-145
New York, NY 10016

Written by/Escrito por: Harold Morris
Translated by/Traducción de: Santiago Ochoa
Spanish-language copyediting and proofreading/Maquetación y corrección en español: Base Tres
Production manager/Coordinadora de producción: Candice Campbell

Photo Credits: Cover photo © Sonsedska Yuliia; background illustration on cover and throughout book © Kannaa; Page 3 © Voren1; Page 4 © ulkas; Page 5 © IRYNA KAZLOVA; Page 7 © Ksenia Merenkova; Page 8 © Eric Isselee; Page 9 © artush; Page 10 © Eric Issele; Page 11 © Nejron Photo (bottom), © cynoclub (top); Page 13 © framsook; Page 14 © Revaphoto; Page 15 © MirasWonderland; Page 17 © Africa Studio; Page 18 © exies; Page 19 © 1stGallery; Page 20 © Chalabala; Page 21 © Smitt; Page 22 © Ljupco, © Artush, © Toloubaev, © anurakpong; Page 23 © Africa Studio, © Chalabala All photos from Shutterstock.com and Istockphoto.com

**Library and Archives Canada Cataloguing in Publication**
Available at the Library and Archives Canada

**Library of Congress Cataloging-in-Publication Data**
Available at the Library of Congress

Printed in the U.S.A./Impreso en los Estados Unidos/CP052026